SPOTLIGHT ON THE RISE AND FALL OF ANCIENT CIVILIZATIONS™

THE TECHNOLOGY OF ANCIENT INDIA

GINA HAGLER

ROSEN
PUBLISHING®

New York

Published in 2017 by The Rosen Publishing Group, Inc.
29 East 21st Street, New York, NY 10010

Copyright © 2017 by The Rosen Publishing Group, Inc.

First Edition

Library of Congress Cataloging-in-Publication Data

Names: Hagler, Gina.
Title: The technology of ancient India / Gina Hagler.
Description: First edition. | New York : Rosen Publishing, 2017. | Series:
Spotlight on the rise and fall of ancient civilizations | Audience: Grades 7-12.
| Includes bibliographical references and index.
Identifiers: LCCN 2016000826| ISBN 9781477789445 (library bound) | ISBN
9781477789421 (pbk.) | ISBN 9781477789438 (6-pack)
Subjects: LCSH: Science--India--History--Juvenile literature. |
Technology--India--History--Juvenile literature. | Indus
civilization--Juvenile literature. | Bronze age--India--Juvenile
literature.
Classification: LCC Q127.I4 H27 2017 | DDC 609.34--dc23
LC record available at http://lccn.loc.gov/2016000826

Manufactured in the United States of America

CONTENTS

THREE ANCIENT CIVILIZATIONS

India is a country with a history dating back to the time of the early civilizations of Egypt and Mesopotamia. From 3000 BCE to the present, several notable civilizations and empires have ruled. Each has had a level of technology that helped it to flourish.

The Indus Valley Civilization (3000–1500 BCE) was a civilization during the Bronze Age. It covered a small portion of the Indian subcontinent near the Indus River. It was known for its agricultural output and metalworking expertise.

The Mauryan Empire (320–185 BCE) was an Iron Age civilization that included a significant portion of the Indian subcontinent. This was made possible in part by the Iron Age tools available to them.

The Gupta Empire (320–550 CE) stretched in a band across the top of the Indian subcontinent. It had advanced technology that made use of breakthroughs in mathematics, astronomy, medicine, and architecture. These advances were precursors to the Information Age technology in use today.

Mohenjo-Daro, which means "Mound of the Dead," was an important city during the Indus Valley Civilization. The societies of ancient India enjoyed sophisticated technologies.

WHAT IS TECHNOLOGY?

Technology is the use of scientific knowledge to solve a practical problem. Technology doesn't have to seem advanced by modern standards to be considered advanced when first introduced. For example, when introduced, the inclined plane was a huge leap forward in technology. So were the lever, the wheel, and the pulley. Each of these simple machines used scientific knowledge (observation) to solve the problem of moving heavy objects. Each of these technological innovations gave the people using them a distinct advantage over those who did not have this technology.

Today, computers and smartphones are types of technology that use scientific knowledge to solve problems of communication and global enterprise. These allow data to be shared and people to collaborate within a single building or around the world. Countries such as India, where people make good use of this digital information technology, have a significant advantage over countries that do not have it available to them.

These items were discovered during the archaeological dig at Mohenjo-Daro. They reveal sophisticated carving techniques and also a glimpse into the ancient civilization.

THE INDUS VALLEY CIVILIZATION

The Indus Valley Civilization (3000–1500 BCE) extended from the coast of the Arabian Sea to the Indus floodplain in what is now Pakistan and northwest India. The civilization was at its peak between 2500 and 2000 BCE. Harappa, Mohenjo-Daro, Mehrgarh, and Lothal were important cities. The Indus Valley Civilization is often viewed as consisting of three periods: Early (5000–4000 BCE), Middle (4000–2900 BCE), and Mature (2900–1900 BCE).

One reason a civilization was able to flourish in this location is that there was a central plan for management of the river and decisions about which crops to grow. There is also evidence of a central plan for the cities. In addition to the central planning, archaeological excavations have revealed that homes in Harappa and Mohenjo-Daro had advanced features such as bathrooms, wells, and sanitation systems. Archaeologists have found remains of a writing system and evidence of trade with other civilizations of the time, as well.

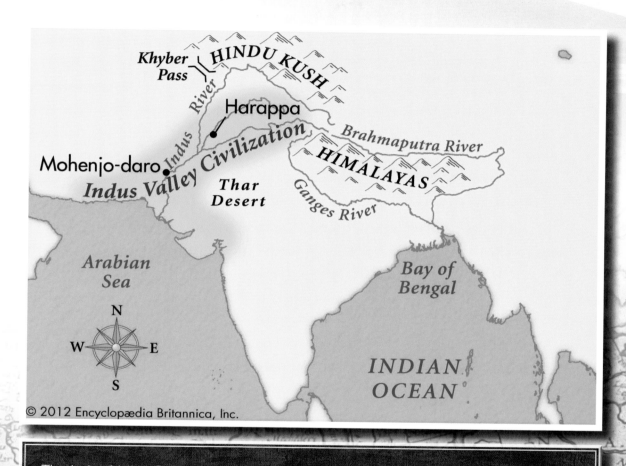

Khyber Pass

HINDU KUSH

Indus River

Harappa

Mohenjo-daro

Indus Valley Civilization

Thar Desert

Brahmaputra River

HIMALAYAS

Ganges River

Arabian Sea

N
W   E
S

Bay of Bengal

INDIAN OCEAN

© 2012 Encyclopædia Britannica, Inc.

The Indus Valley Civilization extended from the coast of the Arabian Sea to the Indus floodplain in what is now Pakistan and northwest India. The Indus River offered water and the fertile soil surrounding it provided food.

TECHNOLOGY OF THE BRONZE AGE

The Indus Valley Civilization was a Bronze Age civilization in which artisans knew how to melt and mix copper and tin to make bronze. It's uncertain where the technology for smelting bronze originated, but there is some thought that it might have come from neighboring areas. Whatever the source, the science was not understood, and what is more likely is that the discovery of the heat required to melt ore came out of the tradition of using kilns, special devices used to heat materials to very high temperatures, to fire bricks and pottery.

The ability to melt ore and blend one with another to form a third was an advanced technology that gave the Indus River Civilization people more materials with which to work when creating objects for decoration and beauty. It also indicates that there was enough leisure time for trial and error. For tools, stone still would have been the first choice because it was harder than bronze.

The people of the Indus Valley enjoyed games, just like we do today. This board game dates back to the Indus Valley Civilization.

BRICKS

It may sound funny to us today, but the introduction of the brick was a significant event in the Indus Valley Civilization. Once the ratio of soil to water to clay was perfected, bricks of different sizes could be made and used for a variety of purposes.

The bricks were strong, too. In fact, many have stood for more than four thousand years. The ratio of soil to clay to water was 1:2:4 for all bricks. That means the mixture was composed of one part soil, to two parts clay, to four parts water.

Once the mixture was ready, it would be poured into a rectangular wooden mold. This was similar to the way that damp sand is packed into a bucket then dumped out to build a sand castle.

Wet bricks would be dried in the sun or in a kiln. When completely dry, the bricks were laid out in rows. Mud was used to "cement" them together to create structures like houses, pavement, and the Great Bath at Mohenjo-Daro.

The great bath at Mohenjo-Daro was technologically advanced for its time. The development of the brick allowed such structures to be built, and to stand the test of time.

SANITATION

The disposal of animal and human waste, especially in cities, was a serious problem for early civilizations. For the people of Harappa and Mohenjo-Daro, a lack of proper sanitation could easily have led to mass deaths. Illnesses such as dysentery or cholera could be caused by waste in the drinking water.

The fact that the people of the Indus Valley Civilization were aware of this and were successful in preventing these problems gave the civilization a great technological advantage over those in the communities around them.

The sanitation system in Harappa and Mohenjo-Daro depended upon a series of drains. These drains led the wastewater to locations that were far from sources of freshwater. There were people tasked with the job of cleaning out the drains and emptying the waste pits. The technological innovation of pipes and covered drains seems simple today but was very advanced for the time.

These covered sewer drains were excavated during archaeological work at Harappa. They are evidence of an advanced technological approach to the treatment of sewage.

WRITING

Archaeologists have discovered more than 3,500 stone seals with more than four hundred different symbols at Indus Valley Civilization sites. The seals are small objects carved out of stone and heated to high temperatures. Most are square with symbols at the top, an animal below that, and more symbols beneath the animal. The back has a place to hold onto the seal while pressing it into other material to make an impression. It seems that some seals may have been worn or carried on a thread.

These seals have been found far outside the Indus River Valley as well. This indicates they may have been used for trading. It seems certain, from comparing the seals with other examples of writing, that the writing on the first line went from right to left, the writing on the second line went from left to right, and on from there.

The use of a written language for shared communication is an important use of technology.

This seal dates back to the time of the Indus Valley Civilization. Seals may have been used for trading, as well as for communication.

THE MAURYAN EMPIRE

The Mauryan Empire (320–185 BCE) was the largest empire ever on the Indian subcontinent. It extended to the north along the Himalayas, to the east into Assam, to the west into what is now southwest Pakistan and southeast Iran, and on into the mountains of what is today Afghanistan. The empire included all but the southernmost tip of the Indian subcontinent. Pataliputra, Tosali, Ujjain, Suvarnagiri, and Taxila were the empire's most important cities.

In its early days, strong rulers and a powerful military maintained order within the empire and extended its reach beyond its boundaries. In the second half of life of the empire, Buddhism became a very important part of the worldview of the leaders and the people.

Technology saw a number of advances during this period. One area of advancement was from Bronze Age to Iron Age metalworking. Others included the refinement of the wheel, improvements in the technology used for roads, and advances in shipbuilding.

This Pillar of Ashoka was erected during the Mauryan Empire. The pillars are carved with edicts by Emperor Ashoka and reflect the importance of Buddhism during the Mauryan Empire.

THE ARTHASHASTRA TEXT

The meaning of the texts of the Indus Valley Civilization may be lost to us, but the text of the Arthashastra is one we can read today. In fact, it is one of the most famous of ancient texts.

The text of the Arthashastra provides a thorough analysis of not only the moral responsibilities of a ruler but also of the ways in which a ruler must protect both himself and his empire through spying and statecraft. It does this by listing seven components of state and twelve levels of relationships with other rulers. It is a brilliant analysis of political thought that includes information on agriculture, manufacturing, and trade.

The Arthashastra text was written in Sanskrit using the ink and materials (technology) of the time. The writing has remained intact for more than two thousand years. The fact that the Arthashastra has been so well preserved is an example of technological sophistication.

This ancient text was inscribed on palm leaves as a writing surface. The messages written upon them can last for up to 800 years.

TECHNOLOGY OF THE IRON AGE

Iron was used most often in the production of tools and weapons during the Mauryan Empire. The ability to take the iron ore and turn it into a form that could be used in the manufacturing of useful objects indicates a high level of technological sophistication. When the Mauryan Empire went up against a society that did not have this technology, it had an advantage.

To get the iron needed from the raw ore, it was necessary to first wash the soil away and then heat the ore to a very high temperature. This resulted in a spongy mass, which could be manipulated but required additional work to shape it. This shaping process required even more heat.

This sort of heat and the introduction of extra oxygen required an advanced technology in the form of furnaces built for this purpose. The Mauryan artisans also improved upon the strength and durability of the iron they produced.

Smelting furnaces were used to produce iron during the Indus Valley Civilization. This furnace was discovered at the archaeological site of Harappa.

REFINEMENT OF THE WHEEL

The rulers of the Mauryan Empire had to protect their vast territory from enemies. To do this required superior weapons, strategic innovation in the placement of men, and the ability to obtain information about their enemies. It also required the ability to move armies quickly both between and across battlefronts in chariots.

The wheel had been in use during the Indus Valley Civilization. Images from that time suggest that the wheel was strengthened by spokes within it.

But a wheel that would bear the weight of a chariot and charioteer needed to be more than very strong. It also had to be true, meaning not distorted in any way that would cause the chariot to veer off course. The wheels for the chariot also had to be identical to one another so that the load would be balanced. If the weakness of one wheel added to the load of another, the chariot would be askew and travel would be compromised.

The wheel had already been invented by the time of the Mauryan Empire, but its design needed to be refined.

ROADS

Marching armies and supplies from one part of the Indian subcontinent to the other was a massive task. The terrain varied across the empire. The ability of the ground to support heavy loads, whether carried on wheels or on animals, depended upon the weather.

The best offense for the Mauryan Empire was to have a network of roads that would provide dependable access to all areas of the empire by any mode of transportation—be it by foot, on animals, or with wheeled vehicles.

The fact that the Mauryan Empire was able to use central oversight and advanced materials to build a network of roads highlights the level of technology available to the rulers of that time. The roads of the Indus Valley Civilization were already paved with brick and ran at right angles. The roads of the Mauryan Empire expanded on that technology to bring the bricks and brick-making technology to the outer reaches of the empire.

The University of Nalanda, pictured here, was constructed by King Ashoka during the Mauryan Empire. The empire's success depended on a vast network of dependable roads.

SHIPBUILDING

For centuries, ships were built through a process of trial and error. Those who needed to travel by water would duplicate what had been done before when building vessels, without any real understanding of gravity, dimensions, or balance.

During the Mauryan Empire, shipbuilding technology continued to advance. There were armies to transport and goods to trade. When these could be sent over water rather than over land, it would cut down on the time required and the wear and tear on the materials, too. Shipbuilding technology advanced to the point that a navy could be maintained and sent as far as Greece, Syria, Egypt, and Macedonia.

Superiority in shipbuilding technology also allowed the Mauryan Empire to have access to gold from regions outside the Indian subcontinent. The ability to trade for goods that would not be readily available on the Indian subcontinent was also a result of the advanced shipbuilding technology.

This frieze created during the Mauryan Empire depicts the importance of water travel during the period. Shipbuilding techniques advanced out of necessity, to increase trade opportunities and extend the reach of the military.

THE GUPTA EMPIRE

The Gupta Empire (320–550 CE) is known as a golden era. This is because during this time art, literature, learning, and trade all flourished. There was peace, ample amounts of food for all, and freedom from widespread death due to battle or illness. Artisans worked in specialized areas to produce goods, and production levels were high enough to provide materials for trade.

The technological advances of the time involved the application of scientific knowledge to questions about the concept of zero and the nature of the universe. Technological advances were also made in medicine and related fields. The architecture of the time reached new levels of refinement. Irrigation and holding tanks continued to be improved.

During the time of the Gupta Empire, the general prosperity and focus on study and knowledge, allowed scientific knowledge and observation to reach new heights. The attitude toward learning and study would remain a part of Indian culture through the coming centuries.

This Temple of Vishnu dates back to the time of the Gupta Empire. During this peaceful and prosperous time, the arts, science, and technology flourished.

MATHEMATICS AND ASTRONOMY

Today we take it for granted that there are nine digits and a zero. We also take it for granted that there is an amount, zero, that indicates there is nothing there. We use Arabic numerals and decimals without wondering where they originated.

These concepts were not always simple, or obvious, to those trying to express amounts through symbols, often over long distances and with people who did not share a common language. The *Aryabhattiyam*, written by Aryabhatta in 499 CE, described many concepts in algebra, arithmetic, and geometry.

We also know today that the Earth spins on an axis and revolves around the sun. We know the length of a solar year; the value of pi; the meaning of a solar and lunar eclipse, and how to predict when one will occur; and the circumference of the Earth. These discoveries were made during the Gupta Empire by Aryabhatta, as well as by an astronomer named Varahamihira.

The Arabic Ciphers.					
European.		Gobar.	Indian.		
14th cent.	12th c.	(Arab.).	10th c.	5th c.	1st c.
1	1	1	9	~	—
2	2	2	?	~	=
3	3	3	3	~	≡
4	8	9	8	y	Ұ
5	9	4	4	ᵫ	ᚼ
6	6	δ	S	G	6
7	7	1	7		ᒋ
8	8	9	C		
9	9	9	ς		
0	0		0	ᒋ	

Aryabhatta developed the concepts of nine digits and zero during the Gupta Empire.

MEDICINE

Surgery was a new concept in ancient India. Setting a broken bone so that it would heal properly was also new. These uses of scientific knowledge to meet a practical need set a higher level for medical technology.

During the time of the Gupta Empire, the use of surgery went beyond simple operations. It included brain surgery and plastic surgery, in the form of reattaching ears that had been cut off. These types of sophisticated surgeries required skill and the ability to control the amount of blood flowing during an operation. They also required the skills to ward off or treat infection after the surgery was complete.

The treatment of illnesses also improved during the Gupta Empire. Doctors had the time and equipment to study the effect herbs had on different conditions. With this knowledge, they could do more than just give comfort to someone who was ill; they could help that person to recover more quickly.

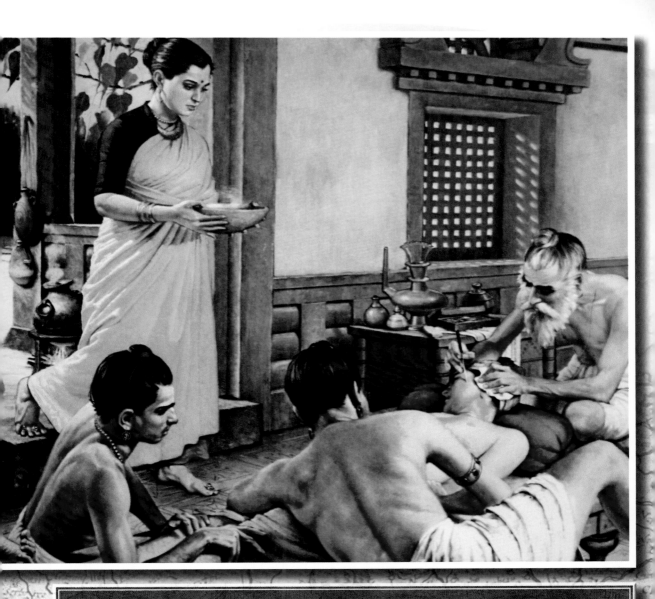

This image depicts Susrutha, a Gupta Empire doctor known as the Father of Surgery, forming an artificial earlobe for a patient.

ARCHITECTURE

The cities in ancient India were designed on a grid pattern for centuries. This was because new civilizations often built their cities upon the ruins of the cities that had come before.

The use of the central plan for a city had other benefits. It helped ensure that the important buildings were located in areas that were accessible to the greatest number of people.

The features of the buildings themselves reflected the technology of the time. In the Gupta Empire, buildings not only had two stories but also featured decorative elements. These included elaborate work on their facades, domes atop the buildings, and polished stones that were used as building materials.

The ability to work with iron was significant as well. A tall iron spire that still stands attests to the abilities of the metalsmiths since this object has withstood time and a variety of weather conditions.

Architecture flourished during the Gupta Empire. Among the many architectural developments include elaborate stone carving techniques on building facades.

IRRIGATION

Droughts were common during the Gupta Empire. Water was such a valuable resource that there was a tax on its use. Water needed to grow crops was delivered through irrigation systems. The systems consisted of dykes to keep the land from flooding and to allow water into canals when the water was needed.

Although simple in theory, in practice this required technology that was advanced for the time. Calculations and construction of an irrigation system could finally bring water to remote areas. The amount of water needed to tend to the gardens of an entire city, along with the needs of the people of that city, demands even more in the way of planning, systems, and oversight.

If one portion of the system failed, the result was a calamity for thousands of people. The ability to manage the dykes, canals, and holding tanks represents a significant level of technology.

Some architectural structures were built as monuments to the gods. Stepwells were water storage tanks that allowed civilizations to reserve water for times of drought and seasonal fluctuations.

INDIA TODAY

Today India is the largest country in South Asia. Seven union territories and twenty-nine states comprise this federal republic. India has a population second only to China. New Delhi is India's capital, and India has fourteen official languages, with Hindi being the most prominent. Although not one of the official languages, English is the most important language for the central government, official communications, and the commercial sector.

Although many technological advances took place during some of ancient India's great empires, technology has waned in modern times. For example, India was not a significant part of the Industrial Revolution.

Today India is developing at a rapid pace. Its stable government, young population, and growing open-market economy—based on the latest technology—makes it possible for India to address long-standing issues such as poverty, discrimination and violence against women, and inadequate access to education for all.

As a developing nation, modern India did not take part in the Industrial Revolution. However, the country has since embraced technology, as evidenced by the numbers of technological workers in India today.

GLOSSARY

Bronze Age The period of time that varies by culture during which tools and weapons were made of bronze, a mixture of copper and tin.

civilization An advanced state of society where a new level of culture, science, and so on has been achieved.

digital The basis of computer technology in which data is expressed as a series of digits with a value of 1 or 0.

empire Vast landholdings made up of state or countries under a single authority.

expertise A high level of competence in an area of knowledge or experience.

floodplain Area of land that is likely to flood, often along the banks of a river or in the lower elevations near a river.

flourish To grow in healthy and vigorous ways, often due to favorable economic or environmental reasons.

Industrial Revolution The period of time that followed the Iron Age, during which powered machines replaced the use of individual hand tools.

Information Age The period of time after the Industrial Age, during which economies are based on the digitization of information.

Iron Age The period of time that followed the Bronze Age, during which tools and weapons were made of iron.

irrigation The application or availability of water for growing crops where there otherwise would not be any.

precursor Comes before, an antecedent of something else.

sanitation The disposal of sewage and other solid waste for purposes of cleanliness and prevention of disease.

subcontinent A subdivision of a continent that is of significant size and largely self-contained.

FOR MORE INFORMATION

Asia Society and Museum
725 Park Avenue (at 70th Street)
New York, NY 20021
(212) 288-6400
Website: http://asiasociety.org/india-historical-overview
The Asia Society is an educational organization with a mission to pro-
mote an understanding of Asian art, culture, business, and policy.
There are offices in Hong Kong, Houston, Los Angeles, Manila,
Melbourne, Mumbai, New York, San Francisco, Seoul, Shanghai,
Washington, DC, and Zurich.

Grameen Foundation
1101 15th Street NW
3rd Floor
Washington, DC 20005
(202) 628-3560
Website: http://www.grameenfoundation.org/where-we-work/asia/india
The Grameen Foundation provides financial and technical support to
microfinance and social enterprises in India. It also works to bring
mobile health initiatives to the people of India through its MOTECH
Platform.

The Indian Archaeological Society
B-17, Qutab Institutional Area,
New Delhi 110 016
India
Website: http://indarchaeology.org/archaeology/archaeology.htm

The Indian Archaeological Society was formed and registered in 1967. Its purpose is to encourage archaeological study of ancient India, as well as the sharing of the findings.

Indian Council of Historical Research
35 Ferozeshah Road
New Delhi 110 001
India
Website: http://ichr.ac.in
The Indian Council of Historical Research was founded in 1972 for the purpose of bringing historians together to conduct and share research into the history of India.

Society for the History of Technology (SHOT)
Department of History
310 Thach Hall
Auburn University, AL 36849-5207
(334) 844-6770
Website: http://www.historyoftechnology.org
SHOT's mission is to support the historical study of technology and the way it relates to politics, economics, and other important aspects of society.

WEBSITES

Because of the changing nature of Internet links, Rosen Publishing has developed an online list of websites related to the subject of this book. This site is updated regularly. Please use this link to access this list:

http://www.rosenlinks.com/SRFAC/itech

FOR FURTHER READING

Avari, Burjor. *India: The Ancient Past: A History of the Indian Subcontinent from c. 7000 BCE to CE 1200*. New York, NY: Routledge, 2016.

Basu, Soma. *Warfare in Ancient India: In Historical Outline*. New Delhi: D.K. Printworld, 2014.

Eck, Diana L. *India: A Sacred Geography*. New York, NY: Harmony Books, 2012.

Holm, Kirsten C. *Everyday Life in Ancient India*. New York, NY: PowerKids Press, 2012.

Kapur, Akash. *India Becoming: A Portrait of Life in Modern India*. New York, NY: Riverhead Books, 2012.

Keay, John. *India: A History: From the Earliest Civilisations to the Boom of the Twenty-First Century*. London: HarperCollins, 2013. Internet resource.

Lassieur, Allison. *Ancient India*. New York, NY: Children's Press, 2013.

Norwich, John J. *Cities that Shaped the Ancient World*. New York, NY: Thames & Hudson Inc., 2014.

Roxburgh, Ellis. *The Mauryan Empire of India*. New York, NY: Cavendish Square Publishing, 2016.

Turner, Tracey, and Jamie Lenman. *Hard as Nails Kings and Queens*. New York, NY: Crabtree Publishing Company, 2016.

Williams, Marcia. *The Elephant's Friend and Other Tales from Ancient India*. Somerville, MA: Candlewick Press, 2014.

BIBLIOGRAPHY

Aronovsky, Ilona, and Sujata Gopinath. *The Indus Valley*. Oxford, England: Heinemann Library, 2005.

Atlas of World History. "Civilization: The Mauryan Empire of Ancient India." TimeMaps Ltd, 2015.

Avari, Burjor. *India: The Ancient Past: A History of the Indian Subcontinent from c. 7000 BCE to CE 1200*. New York, NY: Routledge, 2016.

BBC News. "Indus Valley: Technology and Jobs." BBC, 2014 (http://www.bbc.co.uk/schools/primaryhistory/indus_valley/technology_and_jobs/).

Bowden, Rob. *Settlements of the Indus River*. Oxford, England: Heinemann Library, 2005.

Brain, Marshall, and Robert Lamb. "How Iron and Steel Work." HowStuffWorks (http://science.howstuffworks.com/iron4.htm).

British Museum. "Teaching History with 100 Objects: Seals from the Indus Valley" (http://www.teachinghistory100.org/objects/about_the_object/indus_valley_seals).

Majumdar, R. C. *Ancient India*. Delhi, India: Motilal Banarsidass, 1964.

Mark, Joshua J. "Writing." *Ancient History Encyclopedia*, April 28, 2011 (http://www.ancient.eu/writing).

Mapsofindia.com. "Mauryan Empire" (http://www.mapsofindia.com/history/mauryan-empire.html).

Robinson, Francis. *The Cambridge Encyclopedia of India, Pakistan, Bangladesh, Sri Lanka, Nepal, Bhutan, and the Maldives*. Cambridge, England: Cambridge University Press, 1989.

Spilsbury, Richard. *Settlements of the Ganges River*. Chicago, IL: Heinemann Library, 2005.

Violatti, Cristian. "Arthashastra." *Ancient History Encyclopedia*, 2014 (http://www.ancient.eu/Arthashastra).

INDEX

ABOUT THE AUTHOR

Gina Hagler is the author of many history, science, and technology books for young adults and young readers. She has a lifelong interest in the history of technology and the way technological innovation impacts a society and its rivals.

PHOTO CREDITS

Designer: Michael Moy; Editor: Christine Poolos; Photo Researcher: Bruce Donnola